Your first 100 words in

URDU

Beginner's Quick & Easy Guide to Demystifying Urdu Script

Series concept
Jane Wightwick

Illustrations
Mahmoud Gaafar

Urdu edition
Mohammad Ashraf

Mc
Graw
Hill

New York   Chicago   San Francisco   Lisbon   London   Madrid   Mexico City
Milan   New Delhi   San Juan   Seoul   Singapore   Sydney   Toronto

Audio CD edition
The accompanying CD contains three tracks for each topic:

Repeat and Remember
Speak and Understand
Test Yourself

Topics: 1 Around the House (tracks 2–4), 2 Clothes (tracks 5–7) 3 Around Town (tracks 8–10), 4 Countryside (tracks 11–13), 5 Opposites (tracks 14–16), 6 Animals (tracks 17–19), 7 Parts of the Body (tracks 20–22), 8 Useful Expressions (tracks 23–25), Round-Up (tracks 26–29)

Copyright © 2008 by Gaafar & Wightwick. All rights reserved. Printed in the United States of America. Except as permitted under the United States Copyright Act of 1976, no part of this publication may be reproduced or distributed in any form or by any means, or stored in a database or retrieval system, without the prior written permission of the publisher.

1 2 3 4 5 6 7 8 9 10 11 12 13 14 15 16 17 18 19 20   VLP/VLP   0 9 8 7

ISBN 978-0-07-149873-9 (book & CD set)
MHID   0-07-149873-7 (book & CD set)

ISBN 978-0-07-149874-6 (book part of set)
MHID   0-07-149874-5 (book part of set)

McGraw-Hill books are available at special quantity discounts to use as premiums and sales promotions, or for use in corporate training programs. For more information, please write to the Director of Special Sales, Professional Publishing, McGraw-Hill, Two Penn Plaza, New York, NY 10121-2298. Or contact your local bookstore.

Other titles in this series

Your First 100 Words in Arabic
Your First 100 Words in Arabic, CD edition
Your First 100 Words in Chinese
Your First 100 Words in Chinese, CD edition
Your First 100 Words in French
Your First 100 Words in German
Your First 100 Words in Greek
Your First 100 Words in Greek, CD edition
Your First 100 Words in Hebrew
Your First 100 Words in Hindi
Your First 100 Words in Italian
Your First 100 Words in Japanese
Your First 100 Words in Korean
Your First 100 Words in Korean, CD edition
Your First 100 Words in Pashto
Your First 100 Words in Persian
Your First 100 Words in Russian
Your First 100 Words in Spanish
Your First 100 Words in Spanish, CD edition
Your First 100 Words in Vietnamese

This book is printed on acid-free paper.

◎ CONTENTS

⊚ INTRODUCTION

In this activity book you'll find 100 key words for you to learn to read in Urdu. All of the activities are designed specifically for reading non-Latin script languages. Many of the activities are inspired by the kind of games used to teach children to read their own language: flashcards, matching games, memory games, joining exercises, etc. This is not only a more effective method of learning to read a new script, but also much more fun.

We've included a **Scriptbreaker** to get you started. This is a friendly introduction to the Urdu script that will give you tips on how to remember the letters.

Then you can move on to the 8 **Topics**. Each topic presents essential words in large type. There is also a pronunciation guide so you know how to say the words. These words are also featured in the tear-out **Flashcard** section at the back of the book. When you've mastered the words, you can go on to try out the activities and games for that topic.

There's also a **Round-up** section to review all your new words and the **Answers** to all the activities to check yourself.

Follow this 4-step plan for maximum success:

1 Have a look at the key topic words with their pictures. Then tear out the flashcards and shuffle them. Put them Urdu side up. Try to remember what the word means and turn the card over to check with the English. When you can do this, cover the pronunciation and try to say the word and remember the meaning by looking at the Urdu script only.

2 Put the cards English side up and try to say the Urdu word. Try the cards again each day both ways around. (When you can remember a card for 7 days in a row, you can file it!)

3 Try out the activities and games for each topic. This will reinforce your recognition of the key words.

4 After you have covered all the topics, you can try the activities in the Round-up section to test your knowledge of all the Urdu words in the book. You can also try shuffling all the flashcards together to see how many you can remember.

This flexible and fun way of reading your first words in Urdu should give you a head start whether you're learning at home or in a group.

◎ SCRIPTBREAKER

The purpose of this Scriptbreaker is to introduce you to the Urdu script and how it is formed. You should not try to memorize the alphabet at this stage, nor try to write the letters yourself. Instead, have a quick look through this section and then move on to the topics, glancing back if you want to work out the letters in a particular word. Remember, though, that recognizing the whole shape of a word in an unfamiliar script is just as important as knowing how it is made up. Using this method you will have a much more instinctive recall of vocabulary and will gain the confidence to expand your knowledge in other directions.

The Urdu script is not nearly as difficult as it might seem at first glance. There are 37 letters in total, no capital letters, and, unlike English, words are spelled as they sound. There are two main points to remember:

- Urdu is written from right to left.
- The letters are "joined up" — you cannot "print" a word as you can in English.

◎ The alphabet

The easiest way of tackling the alphabet is to divide it into similarly shaped letters. For example, here are two groups of similar letters. The only difference between them is the dots:

ح (the letter *hay*) ب (the letter *bay*)

ج (the letter *jeem*) پ (the letter *pay*)

چ (the letter *chay*) ت (the letter *tay*)

خ (the letter *khay*) ث (the letter *say*)

When these letters join to others letters they change their shape. The most common change is that they lose their "tails":

$$ ختـ = ح + تـ \qquad بجـ = بـ + ج \qquad $$ (read from right to left) ←

Because letters change their shape like this, they have an initial, a medial (middle) and a final form. For example, the letter ج (*jeem*) changes like this;

- at the beginning of a word (initial) جـ
- in the middle of a word (medial) ـجـ
- at the end of a word (final) ـج

- ✔ Urdu has 37 letters and no capital letters
- ✔ Urdu reads right to left
- ✔ Urdu is written in "joined up" writing
- ✔ The "tail" is generally chopped off before joining the next letter.

A few letters change their shapes completely depending on where they fall in a word. For example, the letter غ (ghain) changes like this:

initial   غٰ   medial   لغٰ   final   لغ

In addition, there are ten letters that never join to the letter following (to their left) and so hardly change shape at all.

و (vao)   ر (ray)   ڑ (Ray)   ز (zay)   ژ (Zay)

ا (alif)   د (dal)   ڈ (Dal)   ذ (zal)   ے (baRii yai)

You will find more details of how the individual letters change their shapes in the table on page 8.

◎ Formation of words

We can use the principles of joining letters to form words. So, for example, the Urdu for farm is written like this

(faarm) فارم = (m) م + (r) ر + (aa) ا + (f) ف ⟵ ─────────

And the Urdu word for "shop" is written like this:

(dukaan) دُکان = (n) ن + (aa) ا + (k) ک + (d) د ⟵ ─────────

You may have noticed that one of the vowels in the word *dukaan* is written above the main script. In Urdu the three short vowels (*a, i, u*) are not written as part of the script but as vowel signs above or below the letters. The short *a* is written as a stroke above the letter (◌َ); the short *i* as a stroke below (◌ِ); and the short *u* as a comma-shape above (◌ُ). This is a similar principle to that used when composing a text message, keying "nxt yr" rather than "next year."

In this book we have included these vowel signs where necessary and the pronunciation guides will also help you. However, most material for native speakers will leave them out and this makes it all the more important for you to start recognizing a word without the short vowels.

✳▲⬓⬚%✳⬩⦂@　هاں　★?✗á✳◆≠❜#?∞

- ✔ Urdu letters have an initial, medial (middle) and final form, depending on their position in the word
- ✔ Many Urdu letters simply lose their tails for the medial and final form
- ✔ A few letters change their shape completely
- ✔ Ten letters don't join to the letter after and hardly change at all
- ✔ The short vowels (*a, i, u*) are written as signs above and below the letter and are not usually included in modern written Urdu

◎ Pronunciation tips

This activity book has simplified some aspects of pronunciation in order to emphasize the basics. Don't worry at this stage about being precisely correct — the other letters in a word will help you to be understood. Many Urdu letters are pronounced in a similar way to their English equivalents, but here are a few that need specific attention:

ص　*(saud)* a strong "s" pronounced with the tongue on the roof of the mouth rather than up against the teeth

ض　*(zuad)* a strong "z" pronounced with the tongue on the roof of the mouth

ط　*(toay)* a strong "t" pronounced with the tongue on the roof of the mouth

ظ　*(zoay)* a strong "z" pronounced with the tongue on the roof of the mouth

ڑ　*(Ray)* a strong "r" pronounced with the tongue on the roof of the mouth

ڈ　*(Daal)* a strong "d" pronounced with the tongue on the roof of the mouth

ح　*(hay)* pronounced as a breathy "h"

خ　*(khay)* pronounced as in "khaki"

ع　*(ain)* this is a sort of guttural "ah" sound

غ　*(ghain)* pronounced in the throat like the French "r" as in "rue"

ء　*(hamza)* strange "half letter," not really pronounced at all, but has the effect of cutting short the previous letter

آ　*(maad)* a long *aa* sound

Another important aspect of Urdu pronunciation is aspirated letters. These letters are spoken with a strong breathy sound. In the Urdu script they are shown by putting ھ after the letter, which is written as an elevated ^{h} in the pronunciation guide:

بھاری (b^{h}aarii) heavy   کھڑکی (k^{h}iRkee) window

Summary of the Urdu alphabet

The table below shows all the Urdu letters, each with its name followed by the pronunciation, and then the letter written independently (Ind.) followed by the three positions. Remember that this just for reference and you shouldn't expect to take it all in at once. If you know the basic principles of how the Urdu script works, you will slowly come to recognize the individual letters.

Name	Ind.	final	medial	initial	Name	Ind.	final	medial	initial	Name	Ind.	final	medial	initial
alif a/u/i/aa	ا	ـا			ray r	ر	ـر			ghain gh	غ	ـغ	ـغـ	غـ
bay b	ب	ـب	ـبـ	بـ	Ray R	ڑ	ـڑ			fay f	ف	ـف	ـفـ	فـ
pay p	پ	ـپ	ـپـ	پـ	zay z	ز	ـز			qaaf q	ق	ـق	ـقـ	قـ
tay t	ت	ـت	ـتـ	تـ	Zay Z	ژ	ـژ			kaaf k	ک	ـک	ـکـ	کـ
Tay T	ٹ	ـٹ	ـٹـ	ٹـ	seen s	س	ـس	ـسـ	سـ	gaaf g	گ	ـگ	ـگـ	گـ
Say s	ث	ـث	ـثـ	ثـ	laam l	ل	ـل	ـلـ	لـ
jeem j	ج	ـج	ـجـ	جـ	sheen sh	ش	ـش	ـشـ	شـ	meem m	م	ـم	ـمـ	مـ
chay ch	چ	ـچ	ـچـ	چـ						noon n	ن	ـن	ـنـ	نـ
Hay h	ح	ـح	ـحـ	حـ	suaad s	ص	ـص	ـصـ	صـ	wao w/o/oo	و	ـو		
Khay Kh	خ	ـخ	ـخـ	خـ	zuaad z	ض	ـض	ـضـ	ضـ	hay h	ہ	ـہ	ـہـ	ہـ
daal d	د	ـد			toay t	ط	ـط	ـطـ	طـ	hamzaa	ء			
Daal D	ڈ	ـڈ			zoay z	ظ	ـظ	ـظـ	ظـ	yay y/ii	ی	ـی	ـیـ	یـ
Zaal z	ذ	ـذ			ain '	ع	ـع	ـعـ	عـ	baRii e/ai yay	ے	ـے	ـیـ	یـ

8

① AROUND THE HOME

Look at the pictures of things you might find in a house.
Tear out the flashcards for this topic.
Follow steps 1 and 2 of the plan in the introduction.

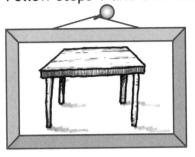

میز mez

ٹیلی ویژن
Taileevizan

کھڑکی k^hiRkee

کُرسی kursee

صوفہ sofaa

کمپیوٹر
kampyooTar

ٹیلی فون
Taileefon

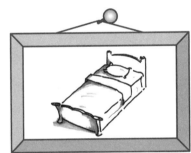

بستر bistar

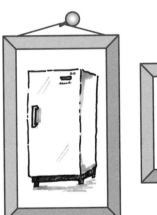

فرتج freej

الماری almaaree

دروازہ
darvaazaa

چُولھا chuulhaa

9

Match the pictures with the words, as in the example.

صوفہ

بستر

کھڑکی

میز

ٹیلی ویژن

کمپیوٹر

ٹیلی فون

کُرسی

Now match the Urdu household words to the English.

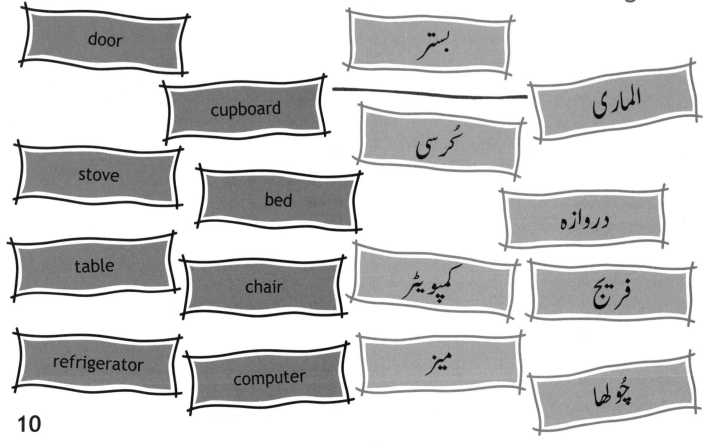

door

cupboard

stove

bed

table

chair

refrigerator

computer

بستر

الماری

کُرسی

دروازہ

کمپیوٹر

فرتِج

میز

چُولھا

Match the words and their pronunciation.

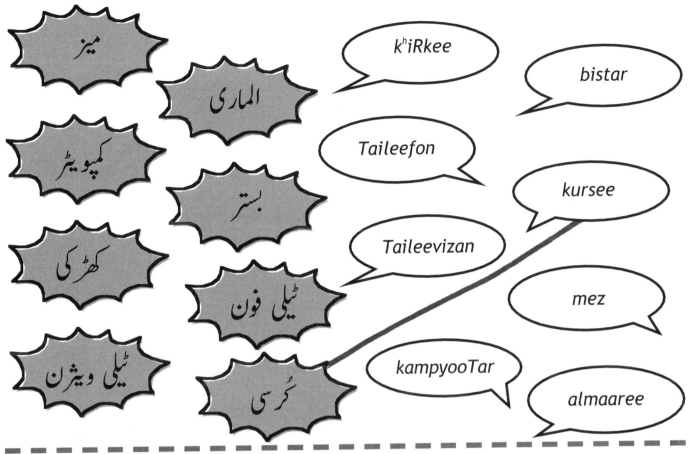

- -

See if you can find six household words in the jumble.

ہوٹل	ٹی شرٹ	قمیض
گھوڑا	چُولھا کھیت بستر	
فرِج	بائیسِکِل دروازہ ریل گاڑی ٹیکسی	
خرگوش	درخت گندا پہاڑی جنگل	
صوفہ	ہلکا مہنگا	
چھوٹا	آہستہ کُرسی بھاری	

11

Decide where the household items should go. Then write the correct number in the picture, as in the example.

4	ٹیلی ویژن	3	صوفہ	2	کُرسی	1	میز
8	چُولھا	7	الماری	6	بستر	5	ٹیلی فون
12	دروازہ	11	کھڑکی	10	کمپیوٹر	9	فرِج

⊚ Now see if you can fill in the household word at the bottom of the page by choosing the correct Urdu.

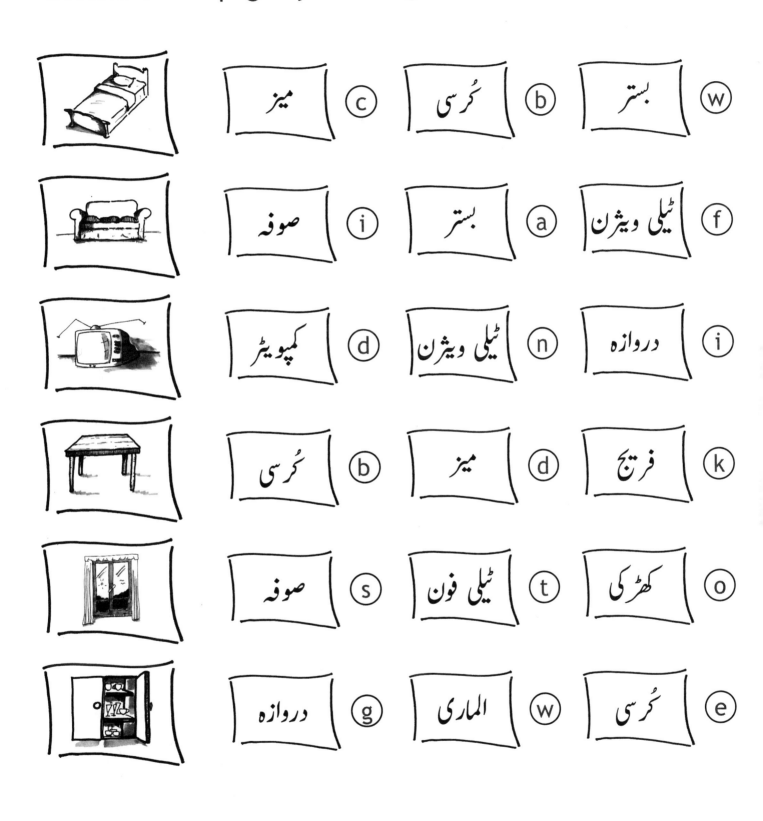

میز ⓒ	کُرسی ⓑ	بستر ⓦ
صوفہ ①	بستر ⓐ	ٹیلی ویژن ⓕ
کمپیوٹر ⓓ	ٹیلی ویژن ⓝ	دروازہ ①
کُرسی ⓑ	میز ⓓ	فرِج ⓚ
صوفہ ⓢ	ٹیلی فون ⓣ	کھڑکی ⓞ
دروازہ ⓖ	الماری ⓦ	کُرسی ⓔ

Εnglish word: ⓦ ◯ ◯ ◯ ◯ ◯

② CLOTHES

Look at the pictures of different clothes.
Tear out the flashcards for this topic.
Follow steps 1 and 2 of the plan in the introduction.

پیٹی peTee

سویٹر swaiTar

جانگھیا jaañgʰiyaa

پتلون patloon

جُراب juraab

ٹی شرٹ Tee sharT

لِباس libaas

ہیٹ haiT

کوٹ koT

سکرٹ skarT

جُوتا jootaa

قمیض kameez

14

Match the Urdu words and their pronunciation.

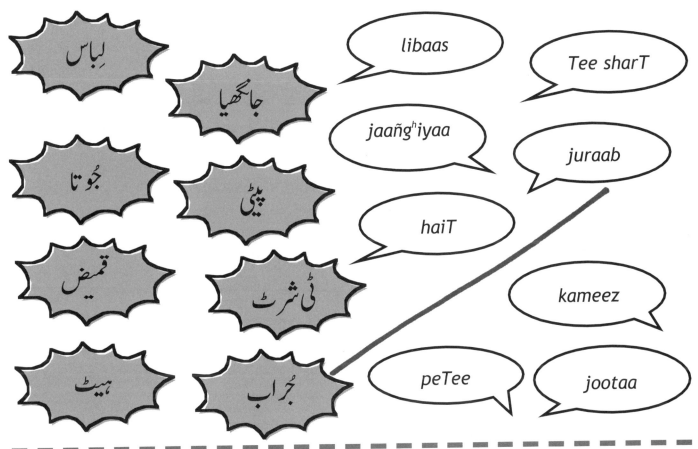

See if you can find these clothes in the word jumble.

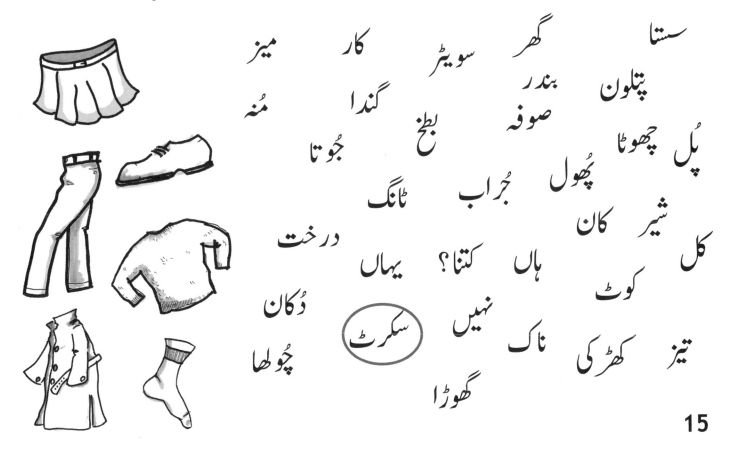

Now match the Urdu words, their pronunciation, and the English meaning, as in the example.

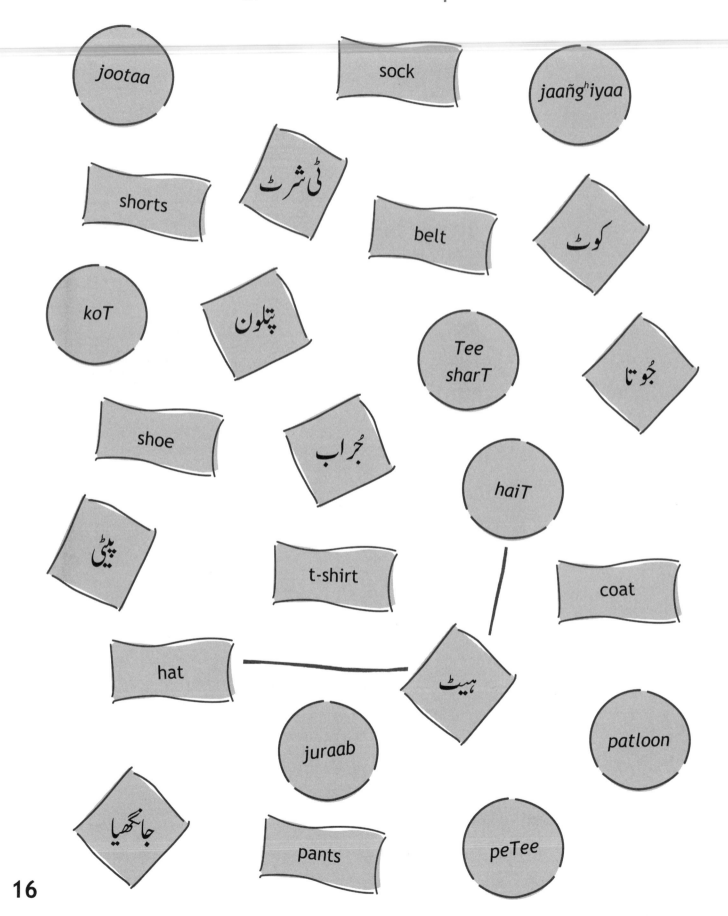

jootaa

sock

jaañgʰiyaa

ٹی شرٹ

shorts

belt

کوٹ

koT

پتلون

Tee sharT

جُوتا

shoe

جُراب

haiT

پیٹی

t-shirt

coat

hat

ہییٹ

juraab

patloon

جانگھیا

pants

peTee

Candy is going on vacation. Count how many of each type of clothing she is packing in her suitcase.

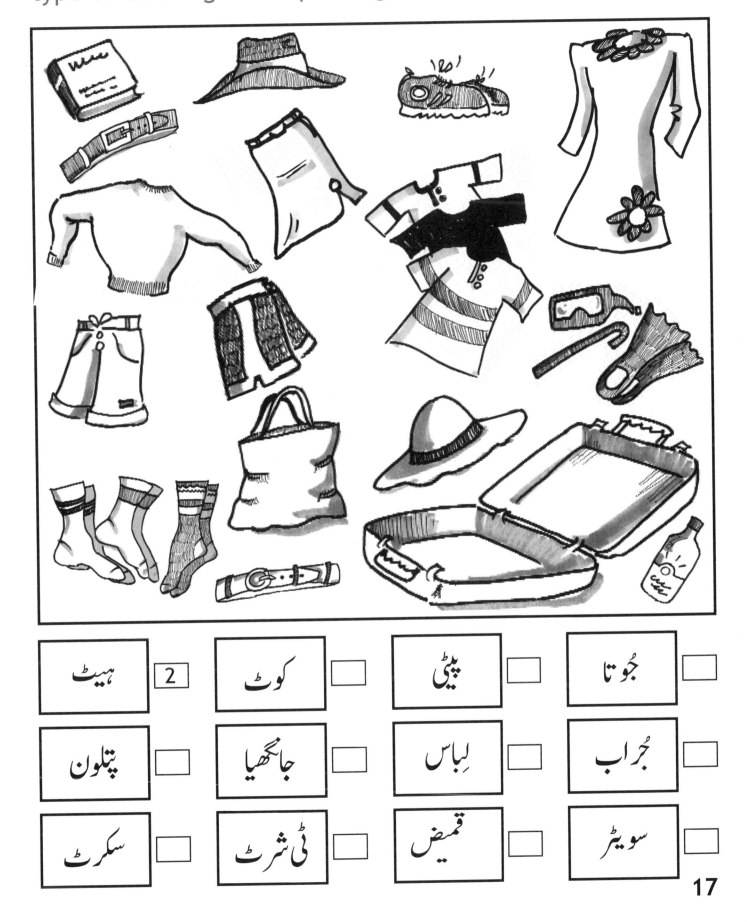

ہیٹ	2	کوٹ		پیٹی		جُوتا	
پتلون		جانگھیا		لِباس		جُراب	
سکرٹ		ٹی شرٹ		قمیض		سویٹر	

Someone has ripped up the Urdu words for clothes. Can you join the two halves of the words, as the example?

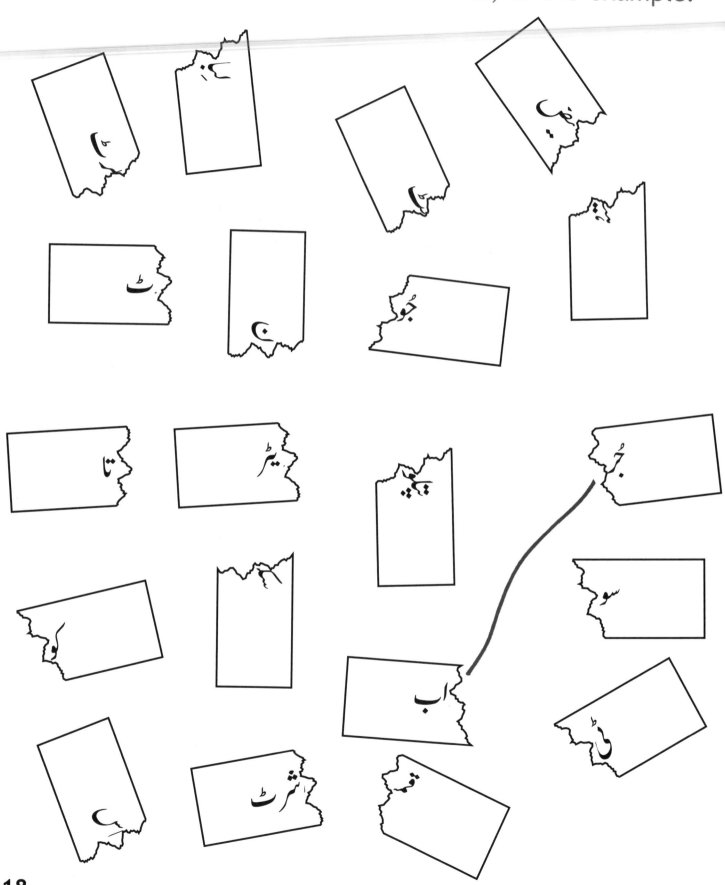

3 AROUND TOWN

Look at the pictures of things you might see around town.
Tear out the flashcards for this topic.
Follow steps 1 and 2 of the plan in the introduction.

ہوٹل hoTal

لاری laarii

گھر gʰar

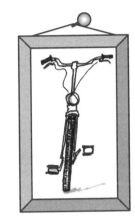

بائیسِکل baaisikal

کار kaar

سینما saneemaa

ریل گاڑی
rel gaaRii

ٹیکسی Taiksii

سکُول skool

سڑک saRak

دُکان dukaan

ریسٹورینٹ
raisTorainT

◎ **M**atch the Urdu words to their English equivalents.

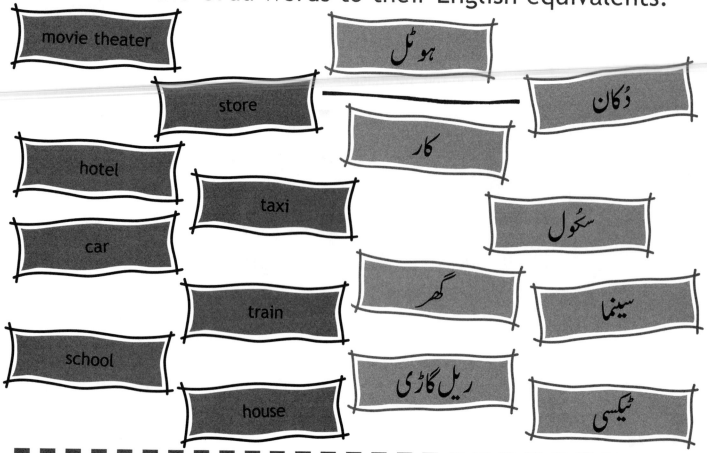

movie theater

ہوٹل

store

دُکان

کار

hotel

taxi

سکُول

car

گھر

سینما

train

school

ریل گاڑی

ٹیکسی

house

◎ **N**ow put the English words in the same order as the Urdu word chain, as in the example.

ٹیکسی | ریل گاڑی | کار | بائیسکل | سڑک | گھر | لاری

bicycle   taxi   house   bus   train   road   car

4   ___   ___   ___   ___   ___   ___

◎ Match the words to the signs.

سکُول   کار   بائیسِکل   لاری

ریسٹورینٹ   ریل گاڑی   ہوٹل   ٹیکسی

Now choose the Urdu word that matches the picture to fill in the English word at the bottom of the page.

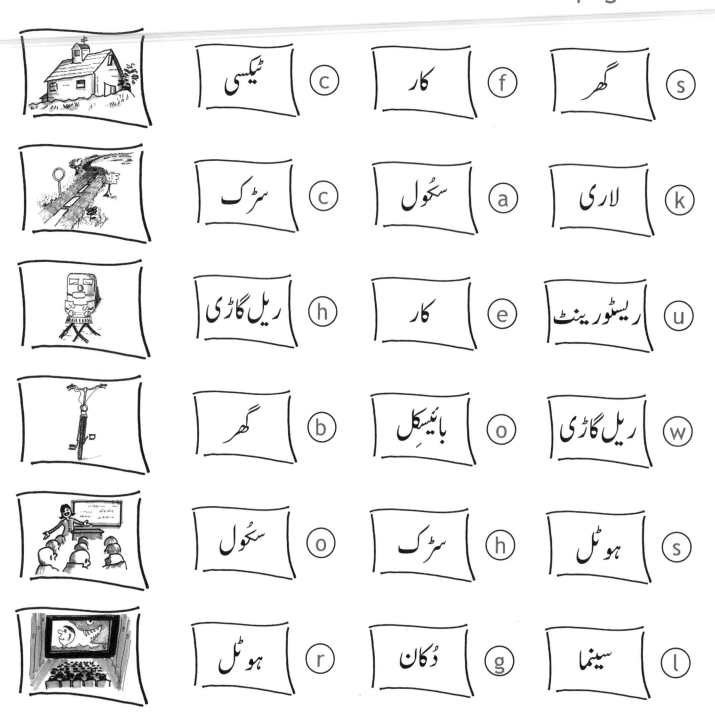

English word: (s) (○) (○) (○) (○) (○)

Now match the Urdu to the pronunciation.

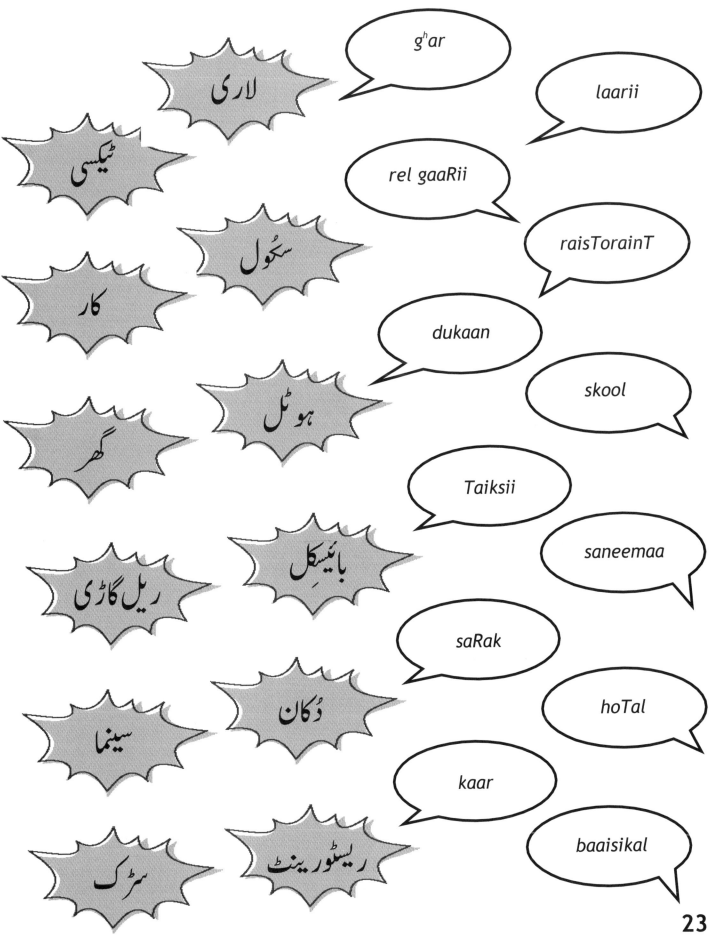

23

④ COUNTRYSIDE

Look at the pictures of things you might find in the countryside.
Tear out the flashcards for this topic.
Follow steps 1 and 2 of the plan in the introduction.

پہاڑی *pahaaRii*

پُل *pul*

فارم *faarm*

پہاڑ *pahaaR*

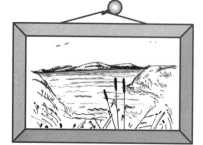

جھیل *jʰeel*

درخت *darakht*

دریا *daryaa*

سمندر *samandar*

پُھول *pʰool*

کھیت *kʰet*

صحرا *sahraa*

جنگل *jangal*

24

Can you match all the countryside words to the pictures.

پہاڑ

فارم

سمندر

جنگل

صحرا

پہاڑی

جھیل

پُل

دریا

پُھول

درخت

کھیت

Now check (✔) the features you can find in this landscape.

☑ پُل	درخت ☐	صحرا ☐	پہاڑی ☐
پہاڑ ☐	سمندر ☐	کھیت ☐	جنگل ☐
جھیل ☐	دریا ☐	پُھول ☐	فارم ☐

26

◎ Match the Urdu words and their pronunciation.

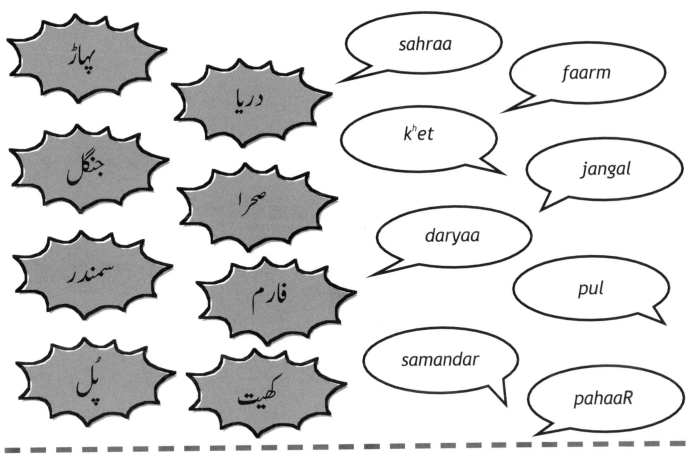

پہاڑ

دریا — sahraa

faarm

kʰet

جنگل

صحرا — jangal

daryaa

سمندر

فارم — pul

پُل

کھیت — samandar

pahaaR

- -

◎ See if you can find these pictures in the word puzzle.

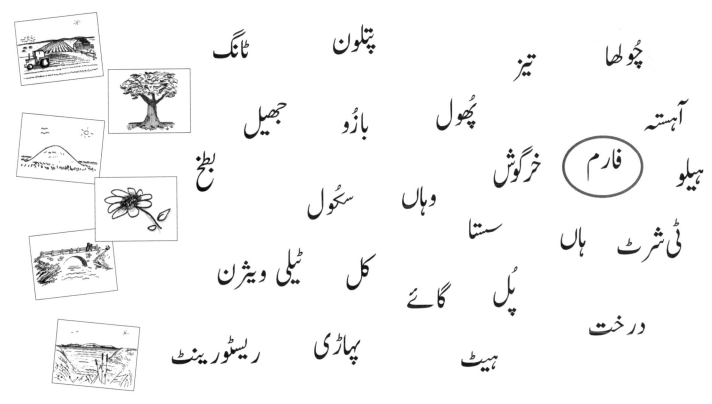

ٹانگ پتلون چُولھا تیز

آہستہ

جھیل بازُو پھُول

ہیلو ‏(‏فارم‏)‏ خرگوش

بطخ

وہاں سکُول ٹی شرٹ ہاں سستا

کل ٹیلی ویژن پُل گائے درخت

ہیٹ پہاڑی ریسٹورینٹ

27

Finally, test yourself by joining the Urdu words, their pronunciation, and the English meanings, as in the example.

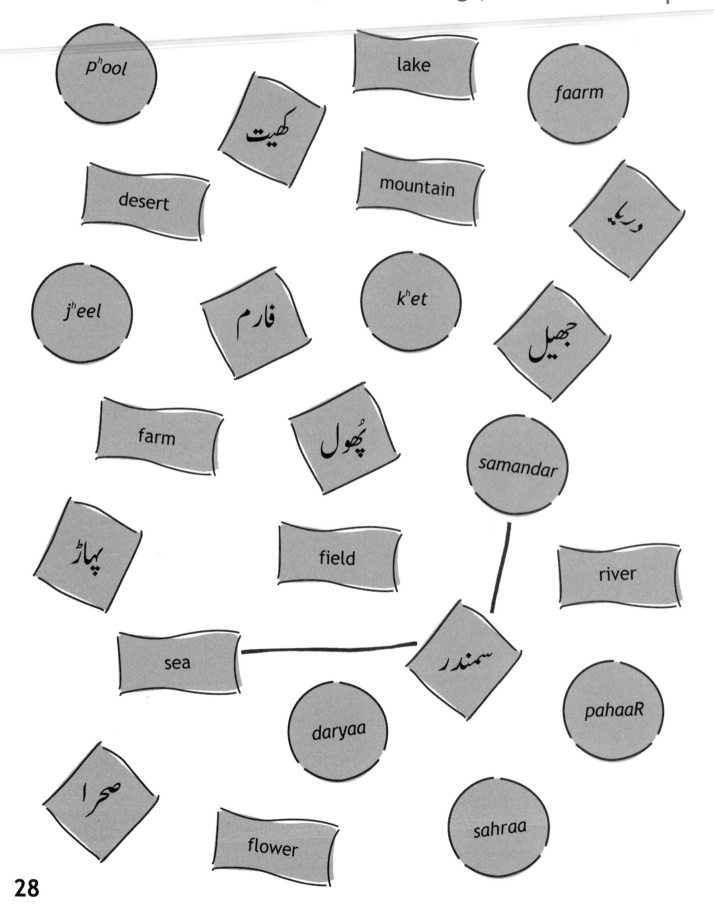

p^hool

lake

faarm

کھیت

desert

mountain

دریا

j^heel

فارم

k^het

جھیل

farm

پھول

samandar

پہاڑ

field

river

sea

سمندر

pahaaR

صحرا

daryaa

flower

sahraa

⑤ OPPOSITES

Look at the pictures.
Tear out the flashcards for this topic.
Follow steps 1 and 2 of the plan in the introduction.

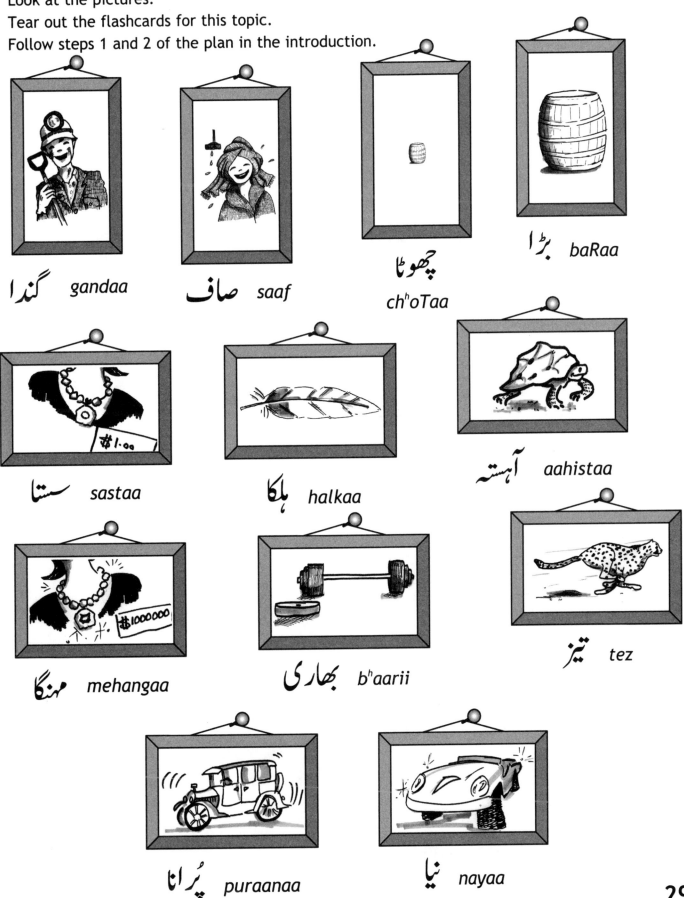

گندا gandaa

صاف saaf

چھوٹا ch^hoTaa

بڑا baRaa

ستا sastaa

ہلکا halkaa

آہستہ aahistaa

مہنگا mehangaa

بھاری b^haarii

تیز tez

پُرانا puraanaa

نیا nayaa

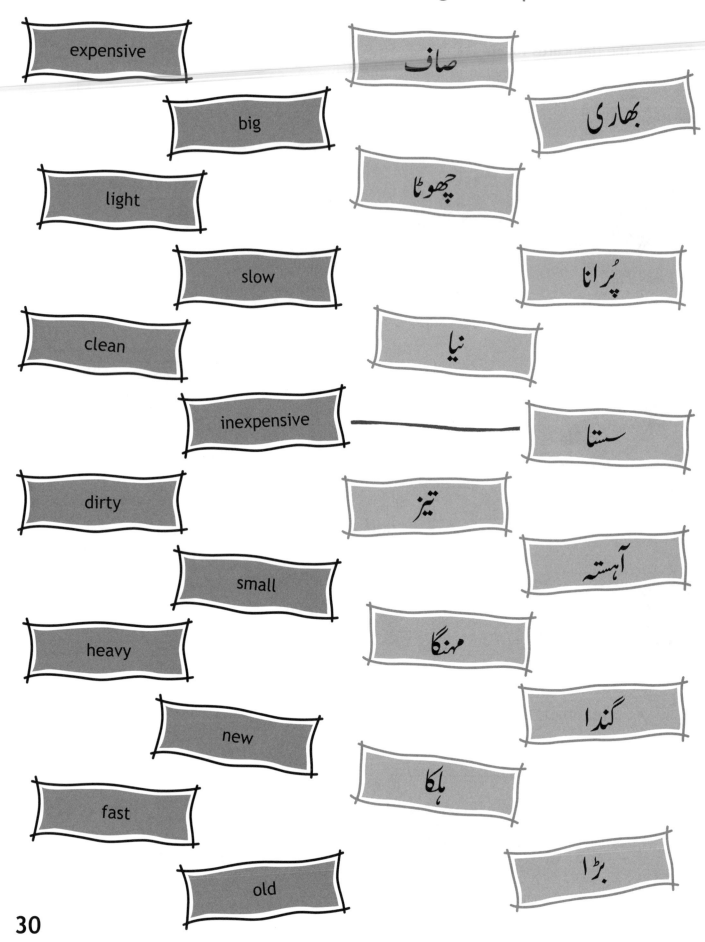

expensive

صاف

big

بھاری

light

چھوٹا

slow

پُرانا

clean

نیا

inexpensive ——— سستا

dirty

تیز

small

آہستہ

heavy

مہنگا

new

گندا

fast

ہلکا

old

بڑا

Now choose the Urdu word that matches the picture to fill in the English word at the bottom of the page.

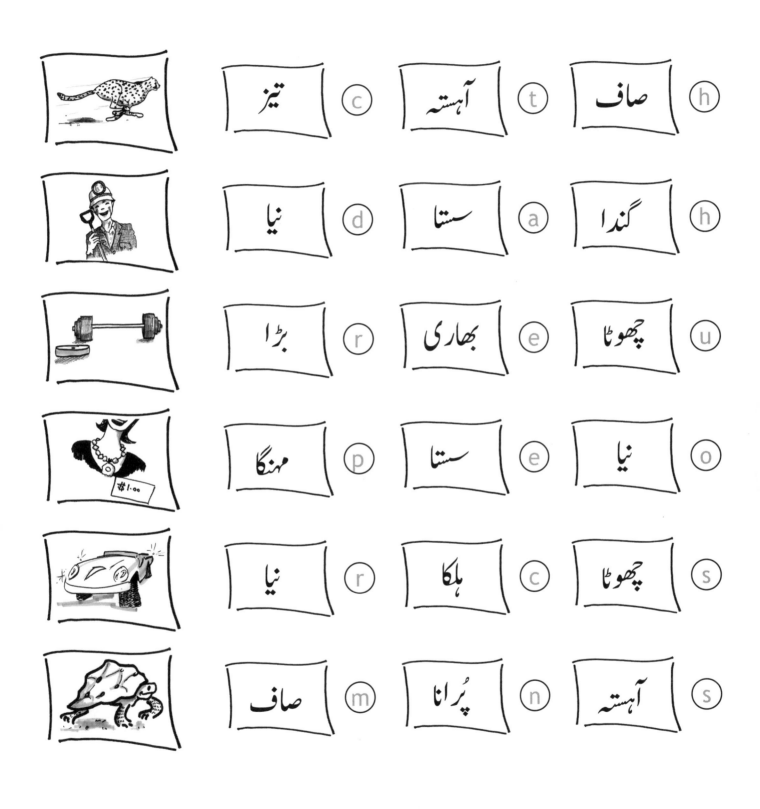

English word: ◯ ◯ ◯ ◯ ◯ ◯ !

Find the odd one out in these groups of words.

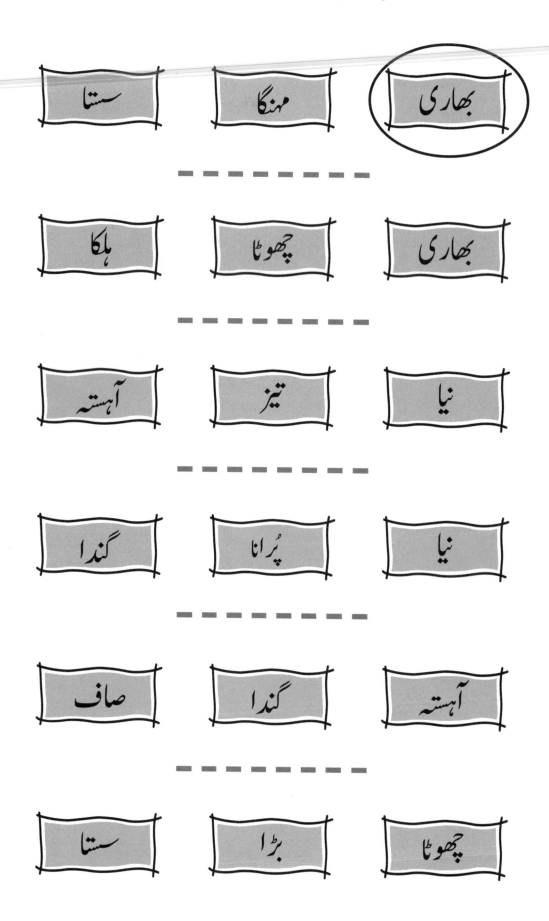

⊙ **F**inally, join the English words to their Urdu opposites, as in the example.

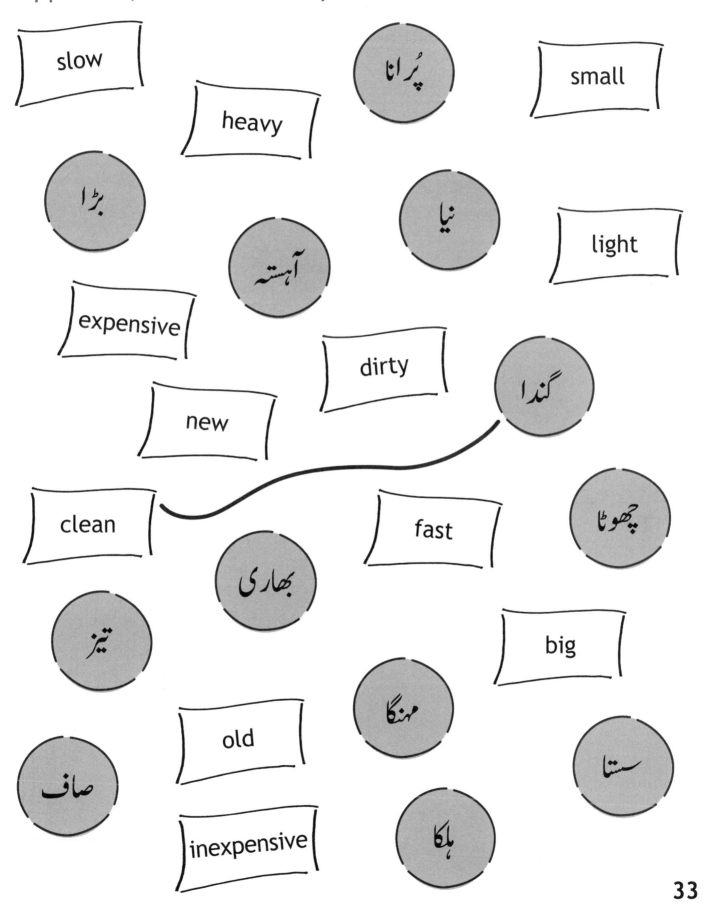

slow

پُرانا

small

heavy

بڑا

نیا

light

آہستہ

expensive

dirty

گندا

new

clean

fast

چھوٹا

بھاری

تیز

big

مہنگا

old

صاف

ستا

inexpensive

ہلکا

33

6 ANIMALS

Look at the pictures.
Tear out the flashcards for this topic.
Follow steps 1 and 2 of the plan in the introduction.

بطخ _batakh_

ہاتھی _haathii_

بلّی _billii_

کُتّا _kuttaa_

خرگوش
khargosh

بندر _bandar_

مچھلی _mach^halii_

بھیڑ _b^heR_

چُوہا _chuuhaa_

گائے _gaaye_

گھوڑا _g^hoRaa_

شیر _sher_

34

Match the animals to their associated pictures, as in the example.

خرگوش

گھوڑا

بندر

بلّی

بھیڑ

چُوہا

کُتّا

گائے

شیر

مچھلی

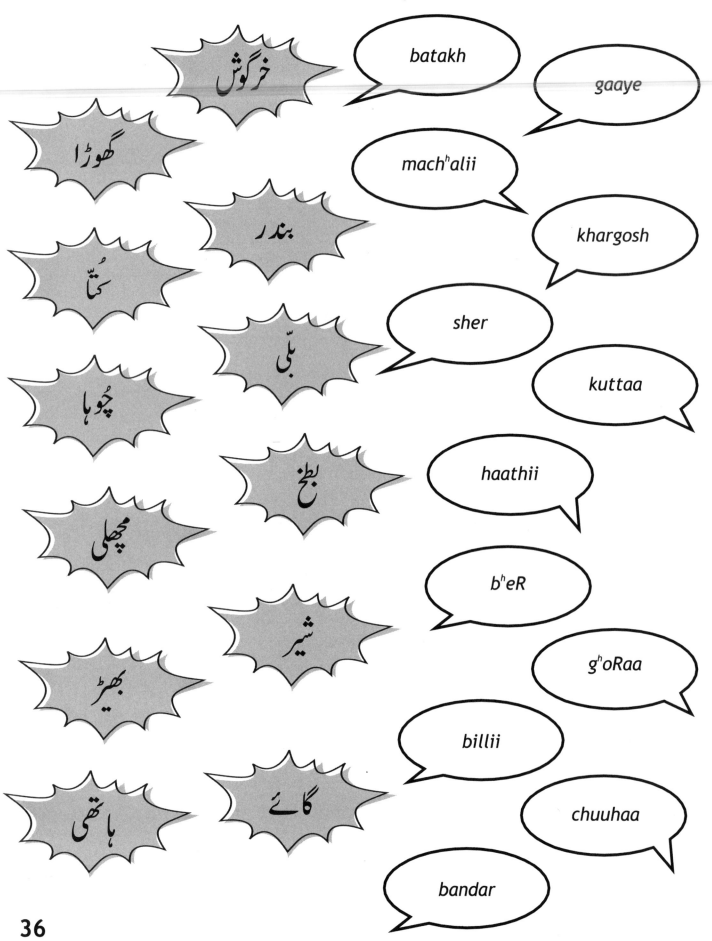

Check (✔) the animal words you can find in the word pile.

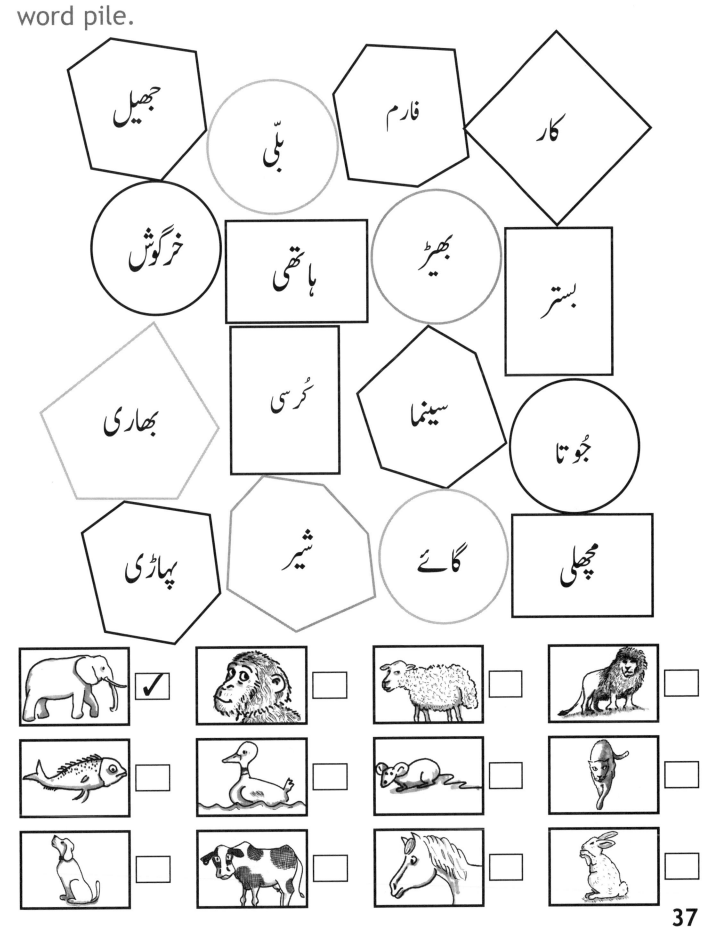

جھیل   بلّی   فارم   کار

خرگوش   ہاتھی   بھیڑ   بستر

بھاری   کُرسی   سینما   جُوتا

پہاڑی   شیر   گائے   مچھلی

Join the Urdu animals to their English equivalents.

monkey

کُتّا

cow

شیر

mouse

بندر

dog

ہاتھی

sheep

خرگوش

fish

مچھلی

lion

چُوہا

elephant

بطخ

cat

گائے

duck

بھیڑ

rabbit

گھوڑا

horse

بِلّی

⑦ PARTS OF THE BODY

Look at the pictures of parts of the body.
Tear out the flashcards for this topic.
Follow steps 1 and 2 of the plan in the introduction.

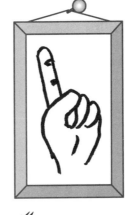

اُنگلی *ungalee*

سر *sar*

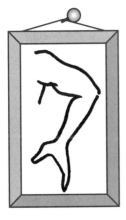

بازُو *baazuu*

آنکھ *aañk^h*

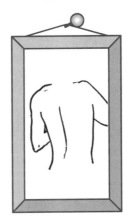

پیٹھ *peeT^h*

ہاتھ *haat^h*

بال *baal*

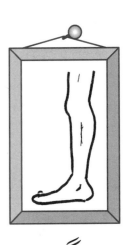

ٹانگ
Taañg

پیٹ *peT*

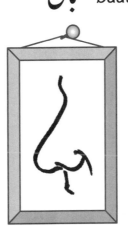

کان *kaan*

ناک *naak*

مُنہ *mooñh*

Someone has ripped up the Urdu words for parts of the body. Can you join the two halves of the word again?

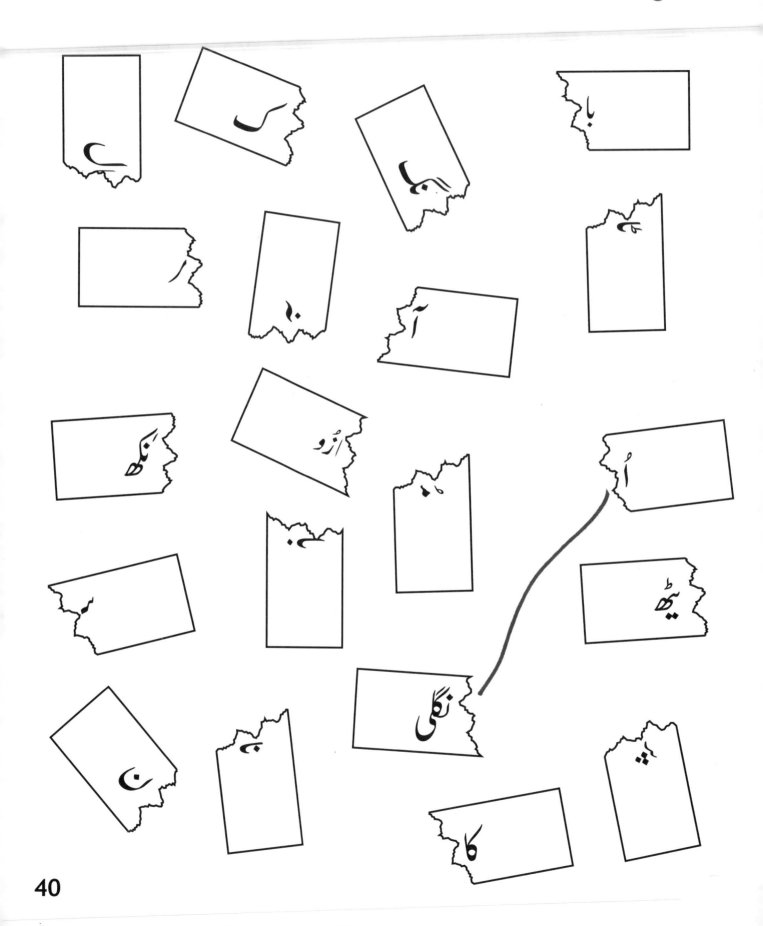

See if you can find and circle six parts of the body in the word puzzle, then draw them in the boxes below.

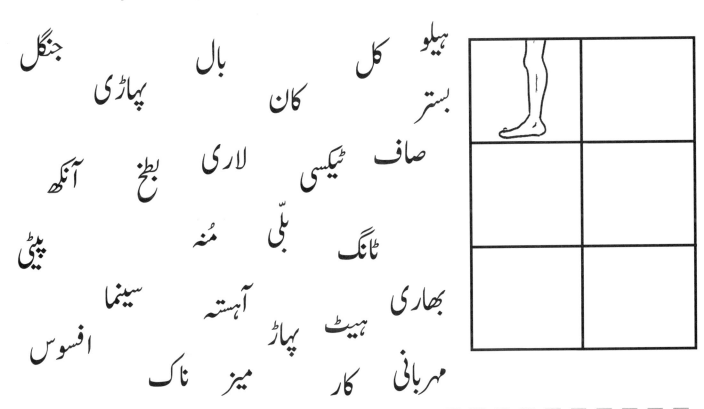

Now match the Urdu to the pronunciation.

© **L**abel the body with the correct number, and write the pronunciation next to the words.

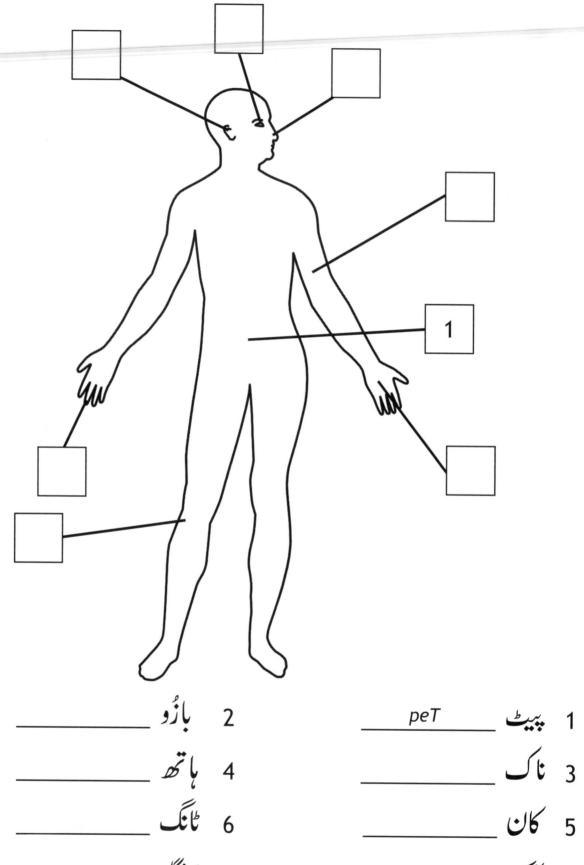

2 بازُو	_____	1 پیٹ	_____peT_____
4 ہاتھ	_____	3 ناک	_____
6 ٹانگ	_____	5 کان	_____
8 اُنگلی	_____	7 آنکھ	_____

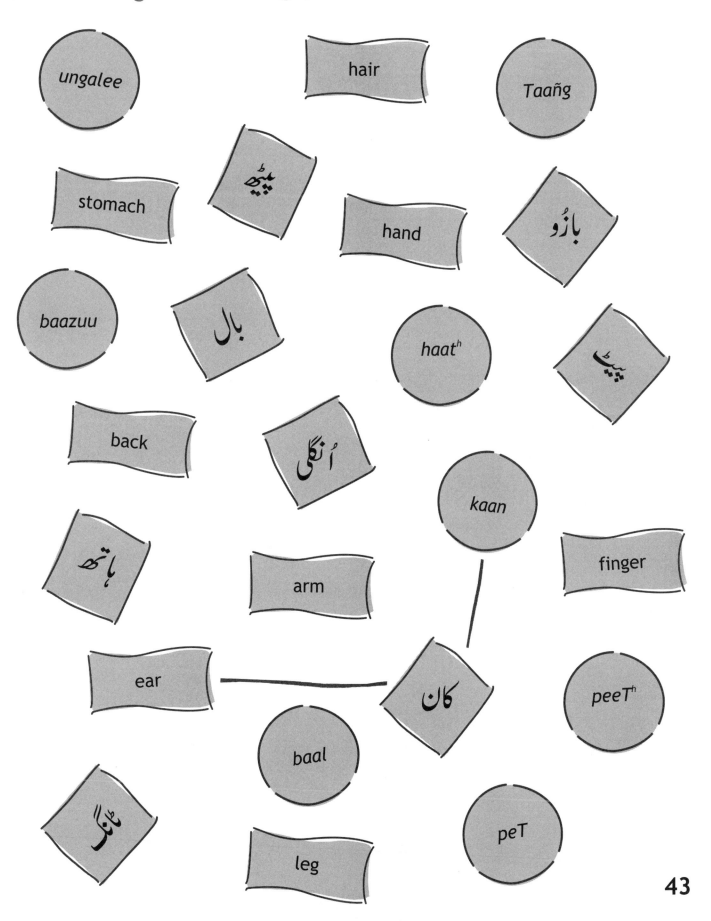

Finally, match the Urdu words, their pronunciation, and the English meanings, as in the example.

ungalee

hair

Taañg

stomach

پیٹ

hand

بازُو

baazuu

بال

haat^h

پیچھے

back

اُنگلی

kaan

finger

ہاتھ

arm

ear

کان

peeT^h

baal

leg

peT

ٹانگ

43

⑧ USEFUL EXPRESSIONS

Look at the pictures.
Tear out the flashcards for this topic.
Follow steps 1 and 2 of the plan in the introduction.

هيلو hailo

خُدا حافظ khudaa haafiz

کہاں ؟ kahaañ

نہیں nahiiñ

ہاں haañ

کل (گُزرا) kal (guzraa)

آج aaj

کل kal

یہاں yahaañ

وہاں wahaañ

اَب ab

کتنا ؟ kitnaa

افسوس afsos

شُکریہ shukriyaa

مہربانی meharbaanii

خُوب khoob

Match the Urdu words to their English equivalents.

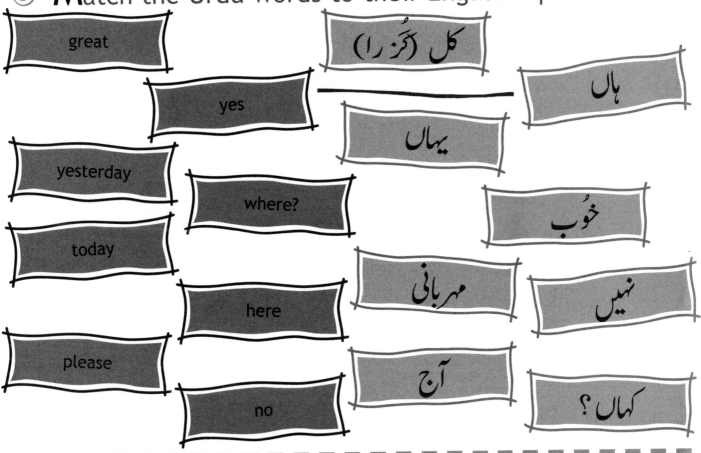

great

yes

yesterday

today

please

where?

here

no

کل (گُزرا)

یہاں

مہربانی

آج

ہاں

خُوب

نہیں

کہاں ؟

Now match the Urdu to the pronunciation.

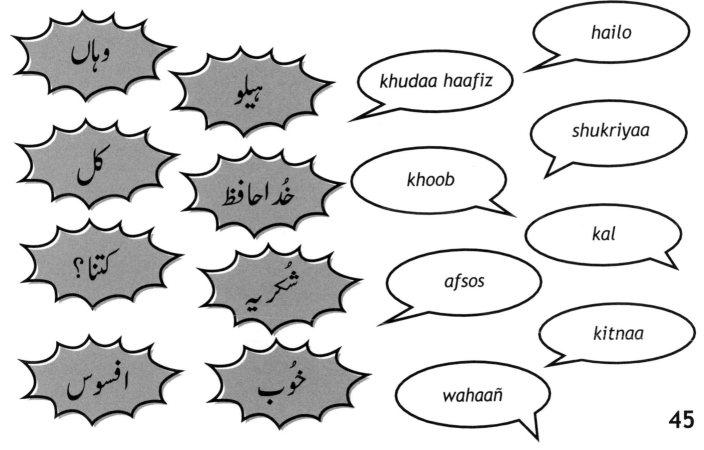

وہاں

ہیلو

خُدا حافظ

شُکریہ

خُوب

کل

کتنا ؟

افسوس

hailo

khudaa haafiz

shukriyaa

khoob

kal

afsos

kitnaa

wahaañ

Choose the Urdu word that matches the picture to fill in the English word at the bottom of the page.

یہاں	p	نہیں	c	ہاں	t
شُکریہ	j	افسوس	a	مہربانی	l
ہاں	m	نہیں	e	آج	i
وہاں	b	ہیلو	a	مہربانی	x
کہاں؟	s	خوُب	h	کل (گُزرا)	t
ہیلو	b	نہیں	y	ہاں	e

Englsh word: ⓟ ◯ ◯ ◯ ◯ ◯

46

What are these people saying? Write the correct number in each speech bubble, as in the example.

4 نہیں   3 ہاں   2 مہربانی   1 ہیلو

8 کتنا؟   7 کہاں؟   6 افسوس   5 یہاں

◎ **F**inally, match the Urdu words, their pronunciation, and the English meanings, as in the example.

shukriyaa

hello

afsos

please

وہاں

thank you

بچے

wahaañ

کل

kal

نہیں

sorry

افسوس

haañ

مہربانی

no

there

yes

ہاں

meharbaanii

hailo

شکریہ

tomorrow

nahiiñ

● ROUND-UP

This section is designed to review all the 100 words you have met in the different topics. It is a good idea to test yourself with your flashcards before trying this section.

- -

◎ These ten objects are hidden in the picture. Can you find and circle them?

دروازہ	پُھول	بستر	کوٹ	ہیٹ
بائیسِکل	کُرسی	کُتّا	مچھلی	جُراب

See if you can remember all these words.

آج

لاری

تیز

ناک

صحرا

ہاں

الماری

شیر

لِباس

سستا

دریا

ٹانگ

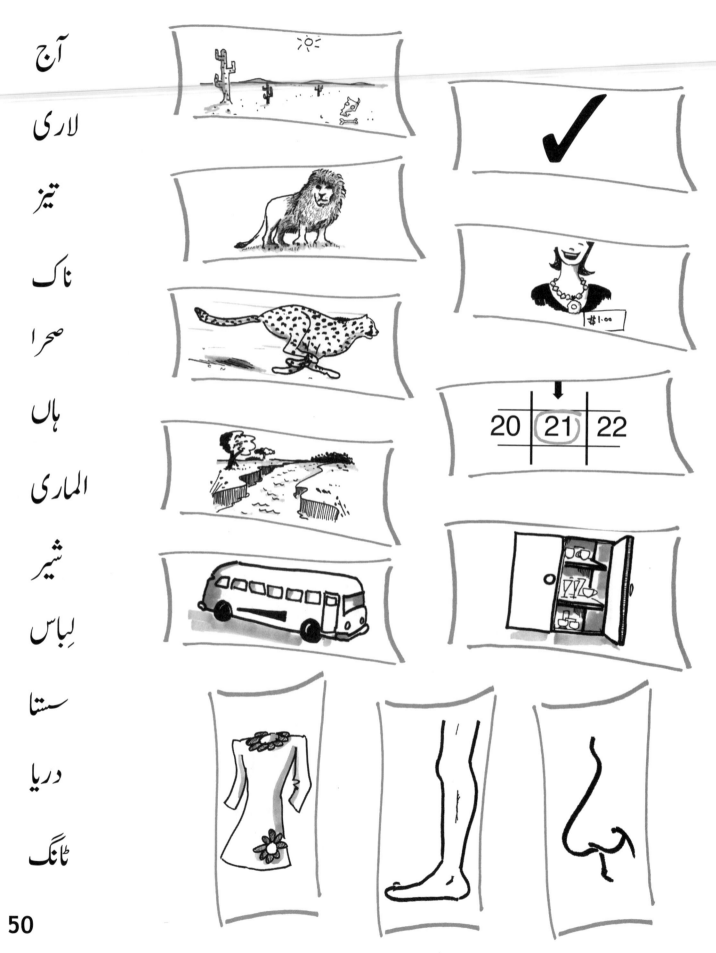

Find the odd one out in these groups of words and say why.

کُتّا	گائے	میز	بندر

Because it isn't an animal.

- - - - - - - -

کار	لاری	ریل گاڑی	ٹیلی فون

- - - - - - - -

فارم	کوٹ	سکرٹ	قمیض

- - - - - - - -

سمندر	جھیل	دریا	درخت

- - - - - - - -

مہنگا	گندا	صاف	سینما

- - - - - - - -

خرگوش	بلّی	مچھلی	شیر

- - - - - - - -

بازُو	صوفہ	سر	پیٹ

- - - - - - - -

مہربانی	کل (گُزرا)	کل	آج

- - - - - - - -

چُولھا	بستر	الماری	فریج

◎ **L**ook at the objects below for 30 seconds.

◎ **C**over the picture and try to remember all the objects.
Circle the Urdu words for those you remember.

پُھول   جُوتا   شُکریہ   دروازہ

کار   نہیں   یہاں   کوٹ   ریل گاڑی

پہاڑ   گھوڑا

پیٹی   سُرسی   ٹی شرٹ   بستر

جُراب   آنکھ

جاگھیا   ٹیکسی   بندر   ٹیلی ویژن

Now match the Urdu words, their pronunciation, and the English meanings, as in the example.

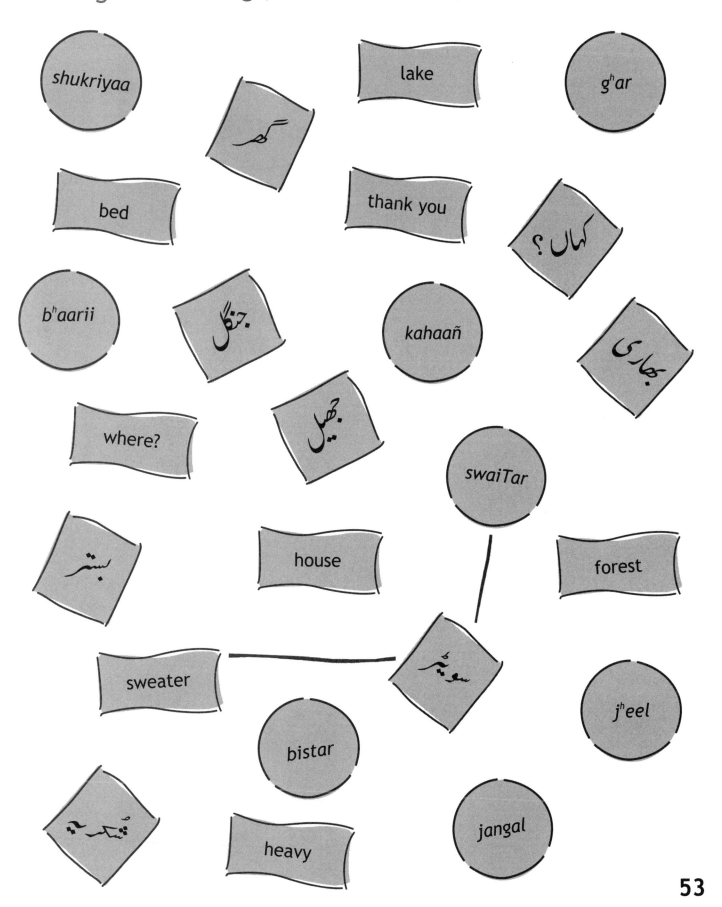

shukriyaa

lake

gʰar

bed

thank you

bʰaarii

kahaañ

where?

swaiTar

house

forest

sweater

jʰeel

bistar

jangal

heavy

صوفہ (w)	ٹیکسی (g)	کان (t)
کوٹ (o)	گندا (a)	پل (e)
ہاں (m)	کتنا؟ (l)	آج (i)
گائے (b)	کھڑکی (l)	ریسٹورینٹ (h)
کہاں؟ (e)	مُنہ (a)	کُتّا (d)
آنکھ (o)	میز (p)	ہیلو (v)
پہاڑی (n)	نہیں (y)	لاری (r)
خرگوش (n)	سٹرک (e)	چُولھا (s)

English phrase: w ◯ ◯ ◯   ◯ ◯ ◯ ◯ !

Look at the two pictures and check (✔) the objects that are different in Picture B.

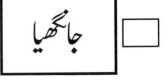

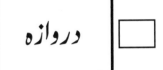

Picture A

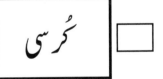

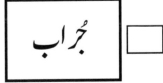

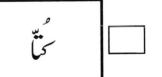

Picture B

refrigerator

بازُو

pants

پیٹ

store

چھوٹا

school

فرِج

river

دُکان

great ———

خُوب

small

دریا

light

پتلون

arm

صاف

stomach

ہلکا

clean

گھوڑا

horse

سکُول

Try to match the Urdu to the pronunciation.

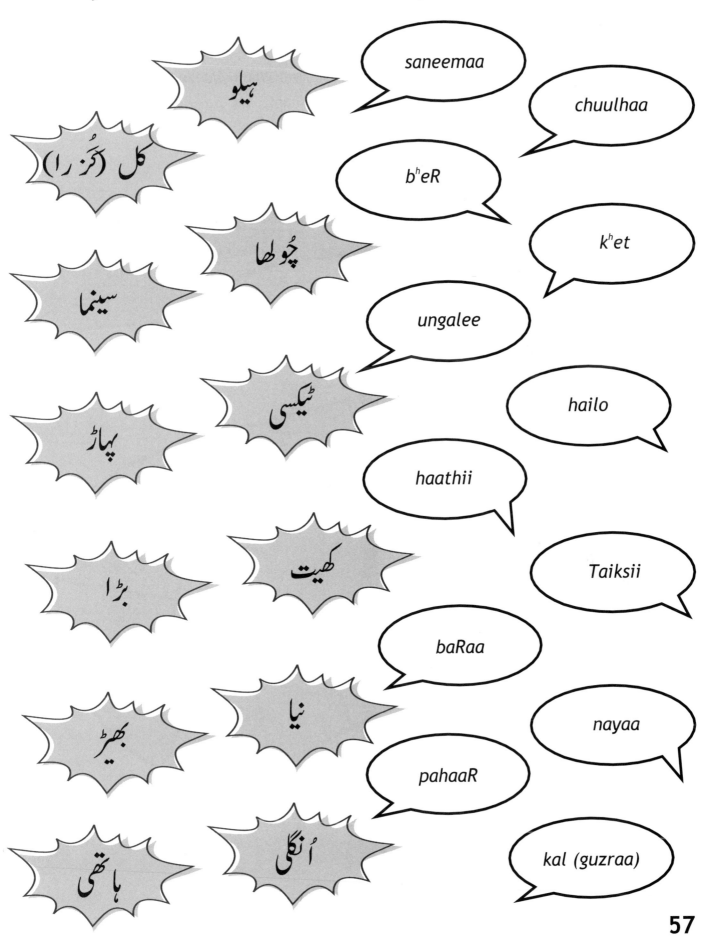

◎ Snake game.

- You will need a die and counter(s). You can challenge yourself to reach the finish or play with someone else. You have to throw the exact number to finish.

- Throw the die and move forward that number of spaces. When you land on a word you must pronounce it and say what it means in English. If you can't, you have to go back to the square you came from.

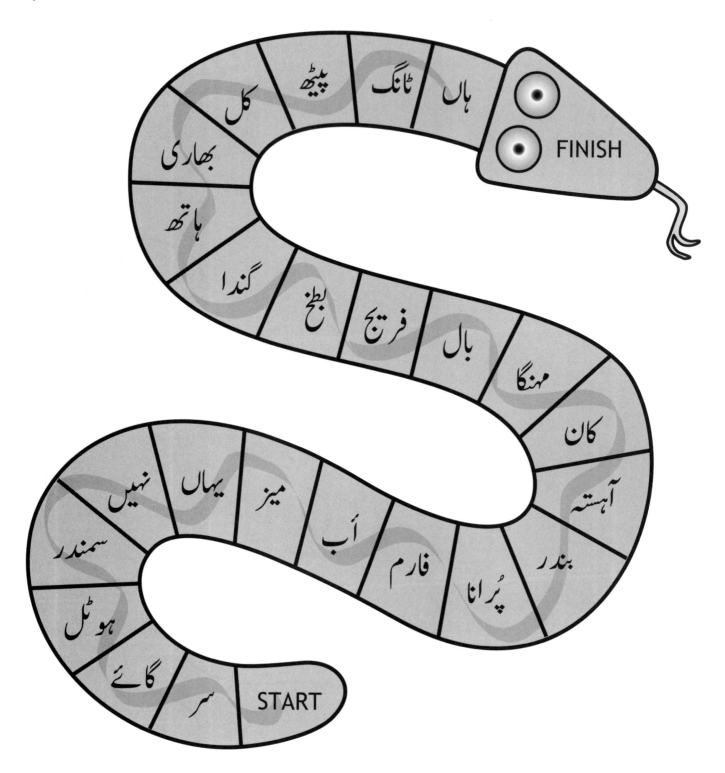

Answers

1 AROUND THE HOME

Page 10 (top)
See page 9 for correct picture.

Page 10 (bottom)

door	دروازہ	table	میز
cupboard	الماری	chair	کُرسی
stove	چُولھا	refrigerator	فرِج
bed	بستر	computer	کمپیوٹر

Page 11 (top)

میز	mez	کھڑکی	kʰiRkee
الماری	almaaree	ٹیلی فون	Taileefon
کمپیوٹر	kampyooTar	ٹیلی ویژن	Taileevizan
بستر	bistar	کُرسی	kursee

Page 11 (bottom)

Page 12

Page 13
English word: window

2 CLOTHES

Page 15 (top)

لِباس	libaas	قمیض	kameez
جانگھیا	jaañgʰiyaa	ٹی شرٹ	Tee sharT
جُوتا	jootaa	ہیٹ	haiT
پیٹی	peTee	جُراب	juraab

Page 15 (bottom)

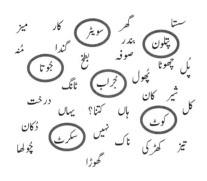

Page 16

hat	ہیٹ haiT	t-shirt	ٹی شرٹ Tee sharT
shoe	جُوتا jootaa	belt	پیٹی peTee
sock	جُراب juraab	coat	کوٹ koT
shorts	جانگھیا jaañgʰiyaa	pants	پتلون patloon

Page 17

ہیٹ (hat)	2	لِباس (dress)	1
کوٹ (coat)	0	جُراب (sock)	6 (3 pairs)
پیٹی (belt)	2	سکرٹ (skirt)	1
جُوتا (shoe)	2 (1 pair)	ٹی شرٹ (t-shirt)	3
پتلون (pants)	0	قمیض (shirt)	0
جانگھیا (shorts)	2	سویٹر (sweater)	1

59

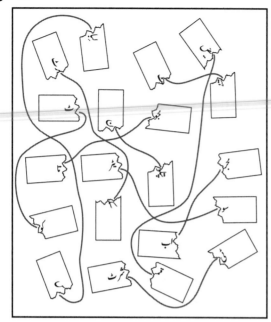

❸ AROUND TOWN

Page 20 (top)

movie theater	سینما	car	کار
store	ڈکان	train	ریل گاڑی
hotel	ہوٹل	school	سکُول
taxi	ٹیکسی	house	گھر

Page 20 (bottom)

bicycle	4
taxi	7
house	2
bus	1
train	6
road	3
car	5

Page 21

Page 22

English word: school

Page 23

لاری	laarii	بائیسِکل	baaisikal
ٹیکسی	Taiksii	ریل گاڑی	rel gaaRi
سکُول	skool	ڈکان	dukaan
کار	kaar	سینما	saneemaa
ہوٹل	hoTal	ریسٹورینٹ	raisTorainT
گھر	gʰar	سڑک	saRak

❹ COUNTRYSIDE

Page 25

See page 24 for correct picture.

Page 26

پُل	✔	کھیت	✔
درخت	✔	جنگل	✔
صحرا	✘	جھیل	✘
پہاڑی	✘	دریا	✔
پہاڑ	✔	پُھول	✔
سمندر	✘	فارم	✔

Page 27 (top)

پہاڑ	pahaaR
دریا	daryaa
جنگل	jangal
صحرا	sahraa
سمندر	samandar
فارم	faarm
پُل	pul
کھیت	kʰet

Page 27 (bottom)

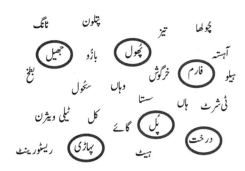

Page 28

sea	سمندر	samandar
lake	جھیل	jʰeel
desert	صحرا	sahraa
farm	فارم	faarm
flower	پُھول	pʰool
mountain	پہاڑ	pahaaR
river	دریا	daryaa
field	کھیت	kʰet

⑤ OPPOSITES

Page 30

expensive	مہنگا		dirty	گندا
big	بڑا		small	چھوٹا
light	ہلکا		heavy	بھاری
slow	آہستہ		new	نیا
clean	صاف		fast	تیز
inexpensive	ستا		old	پُرانا

Page 31

English word: cheers!

Page 32

Odd one outs are those which are not opposites:

نیا	چھوٹا	بھاری
ستا	آہستہ	گندا

Page 33

old	نیا		heavy	ہلکا
big	چھوٹا		clean	گندا
new	پُرانا		light	بھاری
slow	تیز		expensive	ستا
dirty	صاف		inexpensive	مہنگا
small	بڑا			

⑥ ANIMALS

Page 35

Page 36

خرگوش	khargosh		بطخ	batakh
گھوڑا	gʰoRaa		مچھلی	machʰalii
بندر	bandar		شیر	sher
کُتّا	kuttaa		بھیڑ	bʰeR
بلّی	billii		گائے	gaaye
چُوہا	chuuhaa		ہاتھی	haathii

Page 37

elephant	✔	mouse	✘
monkey	✘	cat	✔
sheep	✔	dog	✘
lion	✔	cow	✔
fish	✔	horse	✘
duck	✘	rabbit	✔

Page 38

monkey	بندر	lion	شیر
cow	گائے	elephant	ہاتھی
mouse	چُوہا	cat	بلّی
dog	کُتّا	duck	بطخ
sheep	بھیڑ	rabbit	خرگوش
fish	مچھلی	horse	گھوڑا

❼ Parts of the body

Page 40

Page 41 (top)

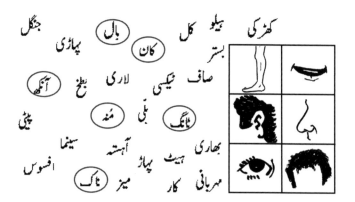

Page 41 (bottom)

سر	sar	بازُو	baazuu
کان	kaan	مُنہ	mooñh
پیٹ	peT	آنکھ	aañk^h
ناک	naak	پیٹھ	peeT^h

Page 42

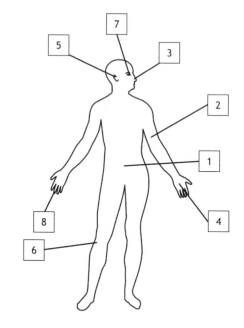

کان	5	kaan	پیٹ	1	peT
ٹانگ	6	Taañg	بازُو	2	baazuu
آنکھ	7	aañk^h	ناک	3	naak
اُنگلی	8	ungalee	ہاتھ	4	haat^h

Page 43

ear	کان	kaan
hair	بال	baal
hand	ہاتھ	haat^h
stomach	پیٹ	peT
arm	بازُو	baazuu
back	پیٹھ	peeT^h
finger	اُنگلی	ungalee
leg	ٹانگ	Taañg

⑧ Useful expressions

Page 45 (top)

great	خُوب	today	آج
yes	ہاں	here	یہاں
yesterday	کل (گُزرا)	please	مہربانی
where?	کہاں؟	no	نہیں

Page 45 (bottom)

وہاں	wahaañ	کتنا؟	kitnaa
ہیلو	hailo	شُکریہ	shukriyaa
کل	kal	افسوس	afsos
خُدا حافظ	khudaa haafiz	خُوب	khoob

Page 46

English word: please

Page 47

Page 48

yes	ہاں	haañ	please	مہربانی	meharbaanii
hello	ہیلو	hailo	there	وہاں	wahaañ
no	نہیں	nahiiñ	thank you	شُکریہ	shukriyaa
sorry	افسوس	afsos	tomorrow	کل	kal

● Round-up

Page 49

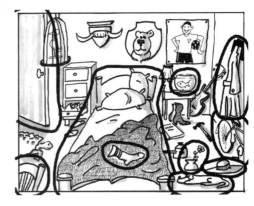

Page 50

Page 51

میز	(Because it isn't an animal.)
ٹیلی فون	(Because it isn't a means of transportation.)
فارم	(Because it isn't an item of clothing.)
درخت	(Because it isn't connected with water.)
سینما	(Because it isn't a descriptive word.)
مچھلی	(Because it lives in water/doesn't have legs.)
صوفہ	(Because it isn't a part of the body.)
مہربانی	(Because it isn't an expression of time.)
بستر	(Because you wouldn't find it in the kitchen.)

Page 52

Words that appear in the picture:

ٹی شرٹ	بندر
کار	ٹیلی ویژن
پُھول	کُرسی
جُوتا	پیٹی
ریل گاڑی	جانگھیا

Page 53

sweater	سویٹر	swaiTar
lake	جھیل	jʰeel
thank you	شُکریہ	shukriyaa
bed	بستر	bistar
house	گھر	gʰar
forest	جنگل	jangal
where?	کہاں؟	kahaañ
heavy	بھاری	bʰaarii

Page 54

English phrase: well done!

Page 55

جانگھیا	✔ (shade)
قمیض	✘
دروازہ	✔ (handle)
بِلّی	✘
کُرسی	✔ (back)
مچھلی	✔ (direction)
جُراب	✔ (pattern)
کُتّا	✘

Page 56

refrigerator	فریج	small	چھوٹا
pants	پتلون	light	ہلکا
store	دُکان	arm	بازُو
school	سکُول	stomach	پیٹ
river	دریا	clean	صاف
great	خُوب	horse	گھوڑا

Page 57

ہیلو	hailo	کھیت	kʰet
کل (گُزرا)	kal (guzraa)	بڑا	baRaa
چُولھا	chuulhaa	نیا	nayaa
سینما	saneemaa	بھیڑ	bʰeR
ٹیکسی	Taiksii	اُنگلی	ungalee
پہاڑ	pahaaR	ہاتھی	haathii

Page 58

Here are the English equivalents of the word, in order from START to FINISH:

head	sar	ear	kaan
cow	gaaye	expensive	mehangaa
hotel	hoTal	hair	baal
sea	samandar	refrigerator	freej
no	nahiiñ	duck	batakh
here	yahaañ	dirty	gandaa
table	mez	hand	haatʰ
now	ab	heavy	bʰaarii
farm	faarm	tomorrow	kal
old	puraanaa	back	peeTʰ
monkey	bandar	leg	haañ
slow	aahistaa	yes	haañ

1

كھڑکی

k^hiRkee

کمپیوٹر

kampyooTar

المارى

almaaree

میز

mez

کُرسی

kursee

فرِج

freej

چُولھا

chuulhaa

صوفہ

sofaa

بستر

bistar

دروازہ

darvaazaa

ٹیلی ویژن

Taileevizan

ٹیلی فون

Taileefon

window	computer
cupboard	table
chair	refrigerator
stove	sofa
bed	door
television	telephone

پیٹی

peTee

کوٹ

koT

سکرٹ

skarT

ہیٹ

haiT

ٹی شرٹ

Tee sharT

جُوتا

jootaa

سویٹر

swaiTar

قمیض

kameez

جانگھیا

jaañgʰiyaa

جُراب

juraab

پتلون

patloon

لِباس

libaas

coat	belt
hat	skirt
shoe	t-shirt
shirt	sweater
sock	shorts
dress	pants

سکُول skool	کار kaar
سڑک saRak	سینما saneemaa
ہوٹل hoTal	دُکان dukaan
ٹیکسی Taiksii	بائیسکِل baaisikal
ریسٹورینٹ raisTorainT	لاری laarii
ریل گاڑی rel gaaRii	گھر gʰar

car	school
movie theater	road
store	hotel
bicycle	taxi
bus	restaurant
house	train

جھیل *jʰeel*	جنگل *jangal*
پہاڑی *pahaaRii*	سمندر *samandar*
پہاڑ *pahaaR*	درخت *darakht*
صحرا *sahraa*	پُھول *pʰool*
پُل *pul*	دریا *daryaa*
فارم *faarm*	کھیت *kʰet*

forest	lake
sea	hill
tree	mountain
flower	desert
river	bridge
field	farm

بھاری

b^haarii

ہلکا

halkaa

بڑا

baRaa

چھوٹا

ch^oTaa

پُرانا

puraanaa

نیا

nayaa

تیز

tez

آہستہ

aahistaa

صاف

saaf

گندا

gandaa

سستا

sastaa

مہنگا

mehangaa

light	heavy
small	big
new	old
slow	fast
dirty	clean
expensive	inexpensive

بطخ

batakh

بلّی

billii

چُوہا

chuuhaa

گائے

gaaye

خرگوش

khargosh

کُتّا

kuttaa

گھوڑا

gʰoRaa

بندر

bandar

شیر

sher

مچھلی

machʰalii

ہاتھی

haatʰii

بھیڑ

bʰeR

cat	duck
cow	mouse
dog	rabbit
monkey	horse
fish	lion
sheep	elephant

بازُو	اُنگلی
baazuu	*ungalee*
سر	مُنہ
sar	*mooñh*
کان	ٹانگ
kaan	*Taañg*
ہاتھ	پیٹ
haatʰ	*peT*
آنکھ	بال
aañkʰ	*baal*
ناک	پیٹھ
naak	*peeTʰ*

finger	arm
mouth	head
leg	ear
stomach	hand
hair	eye
back	nose

شکریہ *shukriyaa*	مہربانی *meharbaanii*
نہیں *nahiiñ*	ہاں *haañ*
خُدا حافظ *khudaa haafiz*	ہیلو *hailo*
آج *aaj*	کل (گُزرا) *kal (guzraa)*
کہاں؟ *kahaañ*	کل *kal*
وہاں *wahaañ*	یہاں *yahaañ*
کتنا؟ *kitnaa*	افسوس *afsos*
اُب *ab*	خُوب *khoob*

thank you	please
no	yes
goodbye	hello
today	yesterday
where?	tomorrow
there	here
how much?	sorry!
now	great!